Vancouver Island Reflections

VANCOUVER ISLAND
Reflections

BY THE PEOPLE OF VANCOUVER ISLAND
AND STUART R. WILSON

Published by the
VANCOUVER ISLAND REAL ESTATE BOARD
Nanaimo, British Columbia, Canada
1976

Contents

Introduction

When Captain Cook landed at Nootka Sound in 1778, the first European to do so, he set in motion a chain of events leading right up to the present and which likely will chart the future of Vancouver Island. Cook instituted a form of trade with the indigenous peoples — sea otter pelts for European knick knacks, in the first instance — that has remained the key to the Island's history ever since.

Trade did not begin with Cook, of course. The Kwagiutl, Nootka and Salish-speaking peoples were themselves great sailors, fishermen, artists and traders who moved restlessly up and down the coast. But the Europeans introduced expanded market opportunities and commerce on a larger scale. And the export economy that developed in Cook's wake, principally staples for manufactured goods, did not spread its benefits equally; some areas of the Island have prospered more than other areas and some peoples have gained what others lost. Vancouver Island nevertheless remains the most beautiful place in the world, so far as I am concerned, and the people who live there are the most fortunate. And though the forces of commerce continue inexorably to guide the Island's destiny, they are perhaps now more than ever before capable of being rationally directed.

A book of this kind is important because it shows how beautiful life on this Island can be, and therefore how important it is for us to exercise that rationality so that the beauty may be preserved and its benefits more fairly enjoyed by all. Those who produced this book are to be congratulated for their contribution to Vancouver Island's future.

M. M. Ames

Michael M. Ames
Director, Museum of Anthropology
University of British Columbia

Aerial view of the Vancouver Island mountains looking west toward Long Beach and the open waters of the Pacific.

Behind the War Canoes

It is a self-contained world.

On the lowlands and huddling at the safe ends of inlets and alongside lakes, one of the world's great primitive civilizations flowered and then was obscured by the culture of the white man.

Winter rain, summer rain, fog and damp. Brisk winds and clear skies. Blistering summer heat in the valleys and on the mountain slopes.

Green in every conceivable shade. Gravel in sombre browns where the rivers course. Grey rock tinged with blue. And in summer brilliant wildflowers and berries. A lush land.

Separated from the world by water, living by the water's edge, dependent on ocean and lake for food, it was here that the Indians of the northwest built the empire of the war canoe. The northern end was occupied by the Kwakiutl tribe. On the central west coast, the Nootkas. To the South, the Coast Salish, a nation that included the Cowichans of the East Coast. This small continent was their homeland.

They worshipped nature: the gods who provided the means of life. Their heraldry was created from nature, but nature as they knew it: bold, often fearsome, vibrant yet moody and brooding.

From the crudest of implements they forged a remarkable culture. The totemic devices remain and are treasured today. But the real measure of the people was the war canoe, giant dugouts which held up to eleven paddlers. With these great canoes, carved from a single cedar tree and then shaped, the Indian people fished, fought and moved entire villages to winter quarters. So great was their skill as seamen that they circumnavigated their island empire long before the white man came. And they pursued and caught great whales in the swells of the North Pacific, then towed them to their villages and feasted.

When the white men finally came, the natives turned traders and brought to that contest skills unmatched in the experience of the early sea captains. Essentially peace-loving people the natives of the island never engaged in open warfare with the white visitors.

While North American folklore is studded with tales of the white men besting indians in battle, in the Land of the War Canoes the story was often reversed. When provoked into a fight, the island's indians won more than their share of the skirmishes, even sinking, burning and capturing visiting armed merchantmen.

Late in the 18th Century when the white man first found this self-contained world, the great names were Cheslakees, Wickanninish, and Maquinna, the latter the greatest chief of them all who forged a massive confederation in order to equalize the contest in trade and in defence. At its height, Maquinna's control encompassed the west coast of the island from Quatsino to Sooke — all of the harbours available to trans-pacific visitors — and even included the tip of the Olympic Peninsula, to block the Strait of Juan de Fuca.

Behind the war canoes came the white man's settlements, industry, farms, mines and government. The indian culture passed into eclipse; the people ravaged by diseases brought by the Europeans. But that culture did not pass without leaving its mark on all of those who came behind. For the indians managed to live in harmony with this land while the white man has often fought nature in an effort to master the land.

Vancouver Island is mountains, trees, and water. Everywhere you turn there is water. Even when one looks to the sky there is likely to be water as the rain clouds are seldom far away.

This is a land of unending growth, constant growth, destructive growth that will obliterate man's works in relatively few years. It is a land that will not be denied.

Once a free indian continent. For several years a land owned and governed entirely by a private

trading organization, the Hudson's Bay Company. Then created the Crown Colony of Vancouver Island it was later merged, in 1858, into a yet larger Crown Colony, British Columbia in an effort to ward off American expansion. In 1871 along with British Columbia, it was taken into the Canadian Confederation to help create a nation from Atlantic to Pacific. Through all this, as today, the island remained solitary, isolated and defiant. And friendly. It is a place of contrasting moods of nature and of people.

An enormous island stretching 282 miles in length it averages sixty miles in width. With 12,408 square miles of territory — well over 13,000 if you include the contiguous islands — it is larger than Belgium or Holland. It is three times the size of Gambia, and somewhat larger than Haiti. All four are independent nations represented in the United Nations while Vancouver Island is now only a Pacific outpost of the world's second largest nation.

Perhaps the best comparison of all is with Taiwan, an island nation of 13,880 square miles and a population of 14,500,000. For all its territory Vancouver Island has a thin population. Most recent estimates place it around 425,000 of which more than half are huddled at the southern tip near the provincial capital, Victoria.

Along the east coast the shoreline and roadways are lined with homes and farms. As you move north, or west, population diminishes; the distance between communities or neighbours grows greater. Almost all the people still cling to the lowlands and inlets as in the days of the indians. For most of this island is mountainous and not arable. On the mountain slopes only the evergreen forests prosper, shielding a rich assortment of wildlife and sometimes hiding mineral wealth.

These mountains, sometimes overlooked except as scenery by the residents who live and work along the lowlands, also are largely responsible for the weather. It is against these mountains that Pacific clouds pile up leaving behind the precipitation necessary for the forests and valleys to thrive. Near the southernmost tip of the island there are no real mountains, rainfall is low and in summer it is a water-short area except where man has interfered. It would be difficult though to contemplate the major portion of the island ever being short of

Dominating the skyline of central Vancouver Island is Mount Arrowsmith. This view is from the Alberni Valley, the only large lowland area not part of the eastern coastal plain.

Completed in 1870, the famous "Butter Church" at Cowichan Bay was built by Father Peter Rondeault but only remained in use for a decade. As well as labouring on the church, the Oblate missionary kept two cows and sold butter to obtain cash with which to buy mortar and other essentials. The Indians of Comaiken laboured with him, quarrying all of the rock used. The sanctuary was restored in 1958 by the Cowichan Indian Band.

At left is a portion of Duncan's Chinatown. Chinese came to the island early in its development, often as labourers to build railwaays and roads, to work in the mines, and later the sawmills. Descendants of those pioneers are to be found in all communities on the island, a reminder that the Orient is also a neighbour separated only by the Pacific.

Opposite Page: Haying time, Cowichan Bay.

water. Apart from the ocean, lakes and rivers are everywhere.

There are really four Vancouver Islands: three geographic and one spiritual. The spiritual island is the land of the native indians, a style adopted to survive both the physical realities of their homeland and its omnipresent moods.

Of the three "geographic" islands, the best known is Victoria, the provincial capital at the southernmost tip of the Island. To Victoria attach the settlements south of the Malahat on the east coast and that portion of the west coast to Port Renfrew that is linked by transport and proximity to the southern tip.

This book is about the other two sections: the developed urbanized central eastern shoreland with its numerous communities and the frontier lands, the west coast and north island areas. Those who live in the cities of the eastern shore

share a lifestyle common to most smaller western Canadian cities but when they seek relaxation it is largely to the outdoors that they turn, to the sea, to the mountains, to forests and lakes.

While the island's modern history was written from the original colonial settlement at Victoria and then north along the eastern shore as men sought first coal, then timber, then gold and other minerals as well as the riches of the sea, the first recorded contact by European explorers was with a part of the island that remains wild to this day: the northwest coast. And that region, now the kingdom of the logger and fisherman, yields a better understanding of the forces that really shape life on Vancouver Island than does the Provincial capital region, for Victoria itself is typical of the island in few respects.

The first recorded certain contact with the outside world came in 1774 when a Spanish sea

15

Ghost communities abound on Vancouver Island. Some were sites of mines, others fishing villages and still others logging or lumbering communities. Port Kusam is near Sayward on the east coast.

St. Mark's Anglican Church at Quamichan near Duncan, has served the settlers of Cowichan valley for over 110 years.

captain Juan Perez recorded sighting the island but did not set foot on it. An early sighting was claimed in 1592 when Juan de Fuca, also with a Spanish expedition, reported discovering the strait which now bears his name.

The Spanish returned under Quadra, Perez and Martinez in the 1780's after Captain James Cook in 1778 had set foot at Nootka claiming the land for the British. In 1789 Martinez seized three British ships at Friendly Cove leading to a dispute between Spain and Britain. A legacy of those early Spanish explorations is more than 200 Spanish place names around the island.

The first white man to live on the island however, was a British ship's doctor, John MacKay, who agreed to winter at Nootka in 1786. He did not enjoy this stay and seemingly lost the friendship of the Indians. He left the following year with Captain Barkley of the *Imperial Eagle*. Accompanying Barkley was his young wife, Frances Hornby, first white woman to visit the island.

That same year, 1787, two American fur traders arrived, Captains Kendrick and Gray, the latter building a fort at Clayoquot.

Only one year later, 1788, Captain John Meares built the first ship to be constructed on this coast, the *North West America*.

Drawing the traders to the Pacific northwest coast were sea otter pelts. So intense did the hunting become that the gentle creatures were nearly exterminated by the turn of the century, a pattern of greed that was to be repeated in later years with sea lions and then with whales.

It was more than half a century later before the forest wealth which built the modern communities of the island attained any prominence. So, too, was general mineral exploration delayed until the middle of the 19th century. It is possible, however, that the Spanish were the real pioneers in mining. Old records indicate they may have found a large amount of gold near Zeballos in 1791.

Journals of those early visitors indicate a rough life offset only by the hopes of making a fortune in the fur-trade. Small wonder, for their attention was concentrated on the island's least hospitable areas. Little attention other than mapping appears to have been paid to the gentler lands across the island.

Even today the sheer size and diversity of Vancouver Island affects people. Those who live in the warmer and drier towns and farming areas underestimate the ruggedness of the other regions while those who live in the damp frontier areas overlook

Standing lonely vigil on the shore of Friendly Cove, Nootka Island, this totem pole shows the beauty of the cedar used in its construction. As cedar weathers in the rain and sun the exterior wood turns silver, lending depth and grace to the carvings as well as a timelessness.

the mild and gentle areas when speaking of the island. Any visitor who has seen only one part of the island or one season leaves with a terribly incomplete conception of its nature.

In mid-summer cloud or rain moving in from the Pacific can drop temperatures to cool levels and up in the mountains they can drop to near freezing levels.

On sunny days temperatures in the valleys can rise to 38°C (100°F). Rain is a constant threat in many areas. In winter snow sometimes reaches down to the seashore, especially on the northern half of the island, but is seldom any problem in the major communities, all of which are at or near sea level and the warming tidal waters.

Dull, damp and sullen on wintry rainy days, the island can suddenly turn bright when the

Above: Old miners cottages at Cumberland provide a reminder of the community's origin in the heyday of the coal mines.

Looking for all the world like a centuries-old farm building in Europe or New England, this abandoned farm shed is near Chase River, south of Nanaimo.

clouds clear. The air is always fresh, alternately wafting the tang of the sea and scent of the forest.

Even on a brilliantly sunny summer day, strong winds can spring up and whistle through the many valleys bringing cool air from the open Pacific waters or snow pockets which remain on the mountains. The smallest lake ripples, then turns into rough water in a short time. On large lakes open stretches of water can readily build up great waves creating a hazard for small boats. So, too, on the ocean where the risk of storm or fog adds to the hazards of the secretive shoals.

On land or water, this country demands respect from those who would seek to know it better. The touches of civilization are still limited in this self-contained world.

Along the roadsides, daisies, dandelions and wild roses bloom together with shrubs of many varieties adding touches and batches of colour

A wedding party takes its leave following a ceremony at Parksville's pastoral St. Anne's Anglican Church, one of the oldest churches in continuous service to upper island residents.

A rose in the chapel reflects the coloration of the stained glass window amid the cool hush of the church's interior. St. Anne's, built of cedar logs, has sheltered worshippers at Parksville since 1894.

to contrast with the infinitely varied greens of the trees and grasses. While driving, patches of brilliant garden flowers growing wild arrest the eye, sown by an enthusiast to relieve the monotony of green and brown or to heal the scars of a roadside embankment.

Off the roadways and along the trails, especially in logged over areas, are found the brilliant chrome yellow of the Tiger Lily in mid-summer, the pink fireweed, scarlet red Indian Paintbrush, and in early summer in some areas giant Rhododendrons native to the Island, with their showy pink blossoms.

Smooth red-barked Arbutus, an evergreen with glossy broad leaves, adds colour to the woodlands of the south island. The Garry Oak adds charm along the southern shores. And along the shore and lower hills in spring and fall the Dogwood bursts forth with its showy white blossoms to prove over and over again why it was selected as B.C.'s floral emblem.

These softer aspects of the land and climate always prevail, generating a love for the island in the hearts of residents and endless enjoyment for the traveller.

Each place in the world has a moment of its own. Vancouver Island's hour is sundown. At sunset Vancouver Island becomes a land of infinite magic ablaze with colour. Yesterday and tomorrow combine as a Cowichan war canoe paddles past the view windows of Wilcuma Lodge overlooking Saltspring Island. One day is ending but the paddlers are preparing for tomorrow. For those who live in this Land of the War Canoes tomorrow is always a day of great promise.

Above: Sailboat, Montague Harbour, Galiano Island.

At right: Indian lady and child at Stewart Bay on Ucluelet Inlet.

21

Undergrowth in the island forests include many varieties of ferns as seen alongside this portion of the trail to Cape Scott Provincial Park. Mature forests (opposite page) have little or no undergrowth.

The Forest Museum at Duncan contains early day and modern logging equipment. A restored logging locomotive takes visitors on a tour of the site. Among the logging techniques pioneered on Vancouver Island was waterbombing of forest fires. Huge Martin Mars bombers, one of which is shown during a test run at their Sproat Lake base, can carry 30 tons of water.

Many of the island's sophisticated forest industry manufacturing plants operate twenty-four hours a day providing nightime sights and sounds. This view is Crown Zellerbach Canada Limited's Elk Falls Paper Mill at Campbell River.

Harbour lights offer a lure all their own. For more than a century trading ships from around the world have called at the island's busy seaports. The chief export is lumber, shown here being loaded at Nanaimo.

An Industrious People

Survival was the first industry of Vancouver Island. The native indians depended on the produce of the forest, sea and lakes for existence.

They harvested the whale, the sea lion and salmon from the deep ocean and collected crabs, clams and oysters near the shore. For oil they collected the oolachan or candlefish, a name derived because it can be dried and used as a torch. To last through winter, salmon was smoked over open fires.

In summer the native indians gathered berries. Their clothing was made of intricately woven bark and of hides. Their homes and canoes of cedar. They traded with inland tribes, bartering oolachan oil for use in lamps against hides. Archaeologists have found artifacts which indicate that there was some ancient contact with the South Pacific and even the Orient. Certainly the natives were experienced in barter when the first white explorers and traders arrived.

The first recorded industry and export of the island is documented in the journals of Captain James Cook in 1778 when he remasted his ships with local timber and traded for sea otter and other pelts as well as obtaining provisions. The furs were sold in the Orient at great profit.

It was the disclosure of Cook's explorations that set Vancouver Island upon its commercial course. Traders followed seeking furs; not only the Spanish and British but American ships out of Boston as well. And they came in numbers.

In 1788 a trader, John Meares, arrived from the Orient and brought home a Nootka warrior, Comekela, brother of Chief Maquinna. In gratitude for his bringing Comekela home, Maquinna permitted Meares to erect a building and Meares later built the first ship constructed on the north coast, the *North West America*. The ship was later lost to the Spaniards during the dispute with Britain over their competing claims to the coast.

The strategic maritime position of the island was to later lead Britain to move its Pacific naval base from Valparaiso, Chile, to Esquimalt at the island's southwestern tip. Other island ports developed facilities for construction and repair of smaller vessels and as industry expanded Cowichan Bay, Nanaimo and Port Alberni grew into significant Canadian seaports with modern facilities and great tonnages of exports. Shipbuilding grew at Victoria and over the years small craft construction and repair facilities developed in the other centres. Modern fibreglas-hulled pleasure craft are now built at Cobble Hill and at Port Hardy and fishing vessels and work boats in several centres.

Among the unusual craft built here are boom boats, an invention native to the island. Created in the 1950's these steel or aluminum-hulled little craft are generally powered by outboard motors fitted through a well in the hull. Highly manouverable they work at high speed, pushing logs from each boom to storage areas or to the mills.

Leading to the naval decision to locate at Esquimalt was of course the earlier creation of Fort Victoria by the Hudson's Bay Company fur traders. Their move from the initial west coast headquarters at Fort Vancouver (now in Washington State) was a reaction to American expansion westward, a decision vindicated when the California gold-rush pulled thousands of men westward and the trek into the Oregon Territories commenced in earnest.

Opposite page: Nanaimo's Bastion, built in 1852 to protect the fledgling settlement against indian attack, has been relocated several times and now stands on a promenade in the city's commercial section overlooking the harbour. A museum occupies the building today and is open to the public.

At that time Victoria was yet a tiny outpost. It was a gold discovery on the mainland which, in 1858, brought thousands of men to Vancouver Island and caused Victoria's population to swell to 8,000. Supplying and transporting the Cariboo-bound miners turned into one of the major activities. It also increased the extent of farming on the south island. Later food products were exported to Alaska, and farming took hold as an important industry on the island.

Expansion of settlement and farming up-island commenced in 1862 when *H.M.S. Hecate* landed a group of 100 settlers at Cowichan Bay not far from the site of the Oblate priest, Father Rondeault's stone "Butter Church". The Cowichan Valley, one of the most fertile on the island, grew slowly and steadily and is now one of the island's most important agricultural areas.

Large and small farms, including a major new Cowichan indian cooperative, produce corn and potatoes as well as the vegetable and berry crops, notably strawberries and raspberries. Holly is yet another export crop of this area. Also important are dairy products, poultry and cattle raising. Milk products alone add some $6,000,000 a year to the economy of the Cowichan Valley.

That pattern of farming is typical of all of the island's low-lying areas and, deltas. The Comox Valley, however, is the only other area where farming is on as large a scale as at Cowichan apart from the original farm area on the rich Saanich Peninsula.

Commerce on Vancouver Island had been expanding and diversifying steadily after the establishment of the first settlement and fur-trading post by the Hudson's Bay Company in 1843. Originally named Fort Camosun, its name was changed to Victoria in 1846. Now the island's largest city and British Columbia's provincial capital, that modern city has a metropolitan population of 222,000 retaining yet its historical connections with England: a connection strongly reflected in its way of life.

In 1849, the same year Vancouver Island was proclaimed a Crown Colony, another fort was established by the Hudson's Bay Company on the northeast coast of the island. The main purpose of Fort Rupert on Beaver Harbour was to protect Scottish miners extracting coal, which had been discovered in 1835, for shipment to Victoria. The mine operated but a short time although the H.B.C. trading post continued until 1873 when it was sold to a former employee who continued to run it for several more years.

Reports of more coal near the indian village of Sne-ney-mo, later Anglicized into Nanaimo, led to the establishment of a mine in 1852 and the first upper-island industry of consequence was genuinely underway. Protecting the fledgling settlement, whose original name meant "meeting of the tribes", was the Bastion, an octagonal-shaped log fort with a planked stockade. A school was built in 1853 and a year later the *Princess Royal* arrived with more than 100 passengers including women, children, a school teacher and more miners from Britain.

In 1862 a new company, Vancouver Coal Mining & Land Company, bought out the Hudson's Bay mine at Nanaimo and increased production, exporting coal to San Francisco. Nine years later Robert Dunsmuir discovered another deposit at Wellington and began to build the first of the fortunes made in island industry.

Other mines followed at Nanaimo, at Comox and Cumberland. The Nanaimo mines drove tunnels under the harbour of the city with shafts rising on Newcastle Island offshore. Dangerous because of gas pockets which collected in the shafts, the mines were often wracked by explosions. The worst occurred May 3, 1887 killing 150 men, an event still marked at Nanaimo with the Bastion flag flying at half mast on that anniversary.

The last of the island coal mines closed in 1966 although deposits remain and changing energy needs may yet see a return of the industry.

In 1847 the British Navy made an effort to obtain spars from Vancouver Island having discovered that trees from the region were longer, straighter and stronger than those the Admiralty was purchasing in the Baltic. Although the original effort was frustrated, it was then to be only a few years before timber moved to the forefront of the island's exports.

The first sawmill was built in 1848 at Esquimalt, now a Victoria suburb, to serve the needs of the growing capital. Sawmilling soon moved up-island with one of the important early sawmills established by Captain Edward Stamp at the head of Alberni Inlet in 1861.

Thirty years later, in 1891, the first paper mill in British Columbia would be established a few miles

Years ago the tallest and strongest straight tree was chosen as a spar tree. Shorn of limbs, they were rigged with cables to pull logs from the woods to a central loading area. Today mobile steel spar trees, like this one shown at Mactush Creek near Port Alberni, offer the added advantage of quick relocation in new cutting areas.

up the Somass River from Stamp's sawmill. That mill, however, was built with used machinery for manufacture of rag pulp and was useless in reducing wood to pulp. After two years of intermittent operation the paper mill closed down, largely due to a shortage of rags. But interest in pulp and paper had been kindled and one of today's great pulp and paper mills is situated on tidewater in Port Alberni. The stones of the original B.C. Paper Manufacturing Co. mill are now on exhibition in Port Alberni.

The forest industry is evident today all over Vancouver Island. It is one of Canada's most important forest production areas with six pulp and paper mills and more than 30 sawmills, plywood and shingle mills in operation.

Railcars loaded with logs and giant trucks hauling logs, plywood, and sawn lumber, and docks crammed with lumber of every dimension at each seaport attest to the scale of forest activity. In British Columbia, fifty cents of every dollar comes from forest wealth. On the island the figure is even higher. But the impact of the industry is not to be measured solely by direct income.

Imaginative men searching for economic production and greater safety have created many of the world's modern forest techniques on the island and then manufactured the necessary equipment. Consequently each community developed a local machine shop to serve local needs. One of these, S. Madill Ltd. at Nanaimo, has grown into a major industrial organization, exporting forestry equipment world-wide, the most famous of which is their steel spar-tree.

The island is also the home of the water bombers, a fire control technique which has since been exported from Canada to many areas of the world. Still flying out of Sproat Lake are the Flying Tankers, giant Martin Mars bombers from World War II re-fitted to carry 30 tons of water scooped from lakes. A retardent is added and the entire 30-ton load is dropped in the effort to control forest

Drilling rig at Utah Mines Ltd.'s Island Copper Mine near Rupert Inlet is shown at right. Over 25 years, pit will attain a depth of 1,000' below sea level. Utah's milling operations (above) adjacent to Rupert Inlet include, left to right, ore stockpile, concentrator, maintenance shop, cone-shaped copper concentrate storage shed, deep-sea dry dock and settling pond. The mine and mill employ 800 people, most of whom live in Port Hardy, 10 miles away.

fires. Those who have seen a "drop" agree that is man's most spectacular fire control technique.

Once a cut-and-run industry, modern forestry technology has replaced that approach with sustained yield methods. Tree seedlings are grown in enormous quantities and some 10,000,000 trees are planted on the island each year. Researchers work to improve the strain and "super trees" of each species are being developed. As long as man needs timber, plywood, pulp, paper and other products of the forest, Vancouver Island's forest-based communities will prosper. Only economic conditions vary capacity to any extent. That stability is the real foundation of the island's prosperity.

Also evident is the fisheries industry. The indians fished for food, as did the early explorers. But the coming of settlements created markets for commercial fishing. The realization of the scale of the fishery in the North Pacific waters soon led to an expanding commercial fishing fleet and fishing villages merged with many of the indian settlements as these often occupied the best sheltered harbours.

The first export, in the 1850's, was salted salmon for the Sandwich Islands. Salmon has remained the chief fishing catch. Cod and halibut are also important commercially while herring, sturgeon, tuna,

sole and other fish are taken. The larger fishing fleets operate out of Port Hardy, Alert Bay, Campbell River, Port Alberni, Nanaimo and Cowichan Bay with one of the most important fleets based in the Ucluelet-Tofino area.

Although less in evidence since the closure of the coal mines, mining and mineral exploration continues to be of economic importance on the island.

Coppers, often breastplate sheets, were wealth symbols among the coast indians. Where they obtained the copper originally has been an interesting question. Originally it appears to have been through trade with Alaskan indians. When the white traders began visiting the coast, sheet copper was among the most valued trade commodities they brought with them.

The great virtue of mining to an economy is that like sophisticated forest industries it is a capital-intensive industry geared to long-term operations and provides stability of employment. Apart from coal, mining on the island has included gold, copper and other metals.

Two significant mines operate today. Island Copper Mine of Utah Mines Ltd. on Rupert Inlet commenced operation in 1971 and employs 800 people. Each year 230,000 tons of copper concentrate and 1,800 tons of molybdenum concentrate are produced for export to Japan. To obtain the 38,000 tons of ore per day capacity, more than $83,000,000 was invested by Utah, an investment justified by estimated reserves of 280 million tons of copper-molybdenum ore.

Mining is by conventional truck and shovel open pit operation, an approach that will, over a 25 year period, create a pit covering some 490 acres and to a depth of 1,000 feet below sea level. Reclamation is already planned and a possibility is a freshwater lake surrounded by campsites. Replanting is underway although the pit proper cannot be touched until mining is complete.

Most of the workers live at Port Hardy where population has jumped from 1,250 in 1969 to nearly 5,000 making it the largest community in the north island area. The recent growth has brought with it new stores, municipal facilities and housing to look after the new residents, thus again repeating the pattern of rapid growth which has marked the history of almost all the island communities.

A second important mining operation is that of Western Mines Limited at the southwest end of Buttle Lake in Strathcona Park. Employing 300, most of whom commute from Campbell River, Western's Lynx and Myra mines commenced operation in 1967. Initially open pit as well as underground operation, the copper, zinc and lead are extracted today almost entirely underground.

Gold, silver and cadmium are also found here. Ore is trucked to Campbell River and shipped by water for smelting elsewhere.

Scattered around the island are many smaller claims some of which have operated at times of

Opposite page: The Gold River Pulp Mill at the head of Muchalat Inlet, one of three arms of Nootka Sound, was built in 1965. There are six pulp and paper mills on the island. Seven miles up river from the mill is the "instant town" of Gold River, built to house the pulp workers. An attractive area, with good fishing, hotel accommodation is available as well as an excellent campsite.

Above: Farming on the island dates back to the arrival of the earliest settlers in the 1840's. Soon after farms were established on the Gulf Islands and along the eastern shoreline of Vancouver Island.

At right: Sturdy tugboats ply the waters around Vancouver Island in all weather pulling barges and booms of logs. Water transport around the island and to the mainland remains an economic and efficient form of transport. Touches of the indian culture show up in many ways on the island, as indicated by this colorful tugboat wheelhouse at Port Hardy.

higher prices or of shortages of certain minerals. Of the now-closed operations, the most famous was Zeballos where gold mining from 1935 until 1948 saw some $6,000,000 produced. Iron deposits at Zeballos, Kennedy Lake and Nimpkish have also produced ore for shipment to Japan in the post-war period and the Benson Lake Mine, operated by Coast Copper Co. near Quatsino, also exported for many years until high production costs and low grade ores forced closure in 1972.

Rumours persist that other ore deposits have a future. One, Falconbridge Mines' Catface Copper near Tofino, reputedly has large deposits awaiting favourable conditions for the building of a 50,000 ton mill. The mountains of Vancouver Island may yet have more treasures waiting to be unlocked. Meanwhile the mining industry has added to road construction on the island and provides a substantial tax base and stable employment for several communities as well as stimulating secondary and service industry growth.

After forestry, the island's largest industry is the travel and recreation industry. Many activities are year-round thanks to the mild climate of the lowlands and seashore. Modern motels and hotels dot the ocean shores and some lakes have long enjoyed the presence of a resort. The earliest was at Shawnigan Lake which remains a popular resort to this day although in later years the area has become better known for a cluster of private schools. Between Shawnigan and nearby Duncan there are now one girls' and four boys' private schools.

But tourism and recreation on the island, while commercially important, are far less visible than other industries and for that matter less noticeable than tourist facilities in most other areas. For the island does not have giant man-made attractions to cater to the visitor. The attractions, and thus the facilities for the visitor, are a part of the warp and woof of island life. Recreation is not just for visitors, it is for everyone.

Abundance of edible fish in adjacent waters has long attracted commercial fishermen to the island. Salmon is the largest catch. Cod, halibut and occasionally tuna are taken. It is a job requiring long hours and patience as symbolized in this photo taken off Tofino.

(Opposite page): Sneaking up on a whale has to be one of the most unusual pursuits available to youngsters anywhere in the world. Giant Basking Sharks, which grow to 50 feet in length, loaf in the sun-warmed waters, especially in Barkley Sound off the Alberni Inlet and each summer fascinate tourists on excursion boats which ply the coastal waters. Gray whales which live along the island's west coast come into the shallow waters and bays to feed.

Whaling, conducted by the indians long before the arrival of white men, became a large industry just before the end of the 19th Century. It petered out after World War II and the last whaling station on Canada's west coast at Coal Harbour (above) closed down in 1970. In recent years researchers have confirmed that whales, largest of the world's mammals, are an intelligent species.

A catch of silver herring, used mainly for bait and fertilizer. One of the tastiest of fishes it is unpopular only because of its many needle-thin bones, a problem easily overcome with a proper recipe.

There's a different island to enjoy in every dawn. Especially along the island's 2,005 mile coastline. Every cove provides a different view, each day a fresh prospect.

"Tofino - 5:00 a.m." captures one such mood; that shared by sport and commercial fishermen who rise early to seek salmon.

The power chain saw revolutionized logging on Vancouver Island. Expert fallers can now bring down a four foot diameter tree in less than one minute. On big trees, notches are carved in the trunk to hold a plank, enabling the fallers to cut above the thicker flaring butt of some trees, especially cedars.

Opposite page:
Modern pulp mills throw vast columns of steam into the air as a reminder that a supply of water is as important as wood itself to pulp and paper manufacture. Shown is the giant Harmac operation of MacMillan & Bloedel near Nanaimo.

By truck, by railcar, by barge and steamship, a continual flow of forest products leaves the island for destinations around the world. Yards like this at Crofton, near Duncan, provide highly efficient storage, sorting and loading facilities.

If there is anything tastier than freshly dug Vancouver Island clams it may be oysters, crab, prawns, shrimps, scallops or abalone prepared ocean-fresh over a campfire, at home or in one of the numerous small restaurants which look after the traveller. Small wonder that the indian people thrived on the island for its waters abound in succulent edible shellfish.

45

Yachts from around the world flock to the island's protected waters. Passing Cortes Island, and a boom of logs, this one may have been returning south after an Alaskan cruise. Adding to the beauty, and the navigational hazards, are rip tides and rapids, such as Arran Rapids at Stuart Island, (opposite page).

Windfalls can make passage alongside island streams, such as Kelvin Creek near Duncan, into a difficult chore. West coast rivers are subject to dangerous flash floods after a steady downpour.

During their annual migrations waterfowl, such as these Canada Geese at Shawnigan Lake, stop-over and use the island's many lakes, ponds and marshes as resting spots.

A Wild and Gentle Land

Vancouver Island is an endlessly fascinating place to explore. Each corner turned, each hilltop surmounted conjures a fresh view. Some are sweeping panoramas. Others, compact jewels obscured from view within a cove or flower-dotted forest glade.

Each prospect itself changes, for this island is a chameleon.

The eye is drawn to and riveted by change. Change here is not just the gradual rotation of seasons shared by all parts of the world, although that too creates effects. Change on Vancouver Island is often momentary. Quick changes in weather alter each scene. A cloudless sky overcasts. A morning haze melts swiftly into the glory of reflecting sunlight. A breeze brushes a scene of total stillness into a motion-filled kaleidoscope of water, forest and sky. Colours blend together creating in real life the fluid impressions of nature's power first shown to the world by painter Emily Carr, a child of the island.

It is a wild land. Yet it is a warm and gentle land. Its beauty never stales. A different world is always but a few steps or a few miles away.

At the northwestern tip of Vancouver Island is a patch of desert-like sand dunes, the most unlikely finishing touch for the visitor from the southern portions of the island and who has travelled overland through seemingly endless forest. This is Cape Scott, most westerly land point and now a provincial park. There is no road to the park. The last sixteen miles from the end of road is by a trail which even in mid-summer is not recommended for use by inexperienced or ill-equipped hikers.

At the western end of Cameron Lake, in the heart of the island, is MacMillan Park with its world-famed Cathedral Grove. A magnificent stand of Douglas Firs spared by the loggers, Cathedral Grove rivals the Sequoia redwood forests of California in size and glory. Amid centuries-old trees towering to 300 feet, a sense of awe is unavoidable. The spiritual impact of the original virgin forests of the island on the indian residents becomes more understandable.

Further south in the gentle Cowichan Valley, a river wends its way through miles of flatland towards a rendezvous with the sea. Along the banks are fields and trails; as well as farms, on which youngsters may canter on horseback, for riding is a popular island pastime.

Hard against the valleys rise the mountains of the island. In one view peaks inaccessible to all but skilled climbers can share a horizon with shoreline, wheat field and city. The temptation to discover such delights seduces everyone away from a fireside and onto a highway, trail or ocean path.

The north island, least well known to islanders and visitors alike, offers many attractions. Winter Harbour, a small logging and fishing community, is but one example. Isolated by its distance from the main settlements and the lack of road access until recent years, Winter Harbour is located on Forward Inlet at the entrance to Quatsino Sound, one of the many beautiful inlets along the Coast.

Once the site of a Kwaksistah village, traces of that history can still be found. A small campsite and park alongside the shingled beach is a thoughtfully chosen spot. Long ago indians hacked down two giant cedar trees, about five feet through, to dig out canoes from the trunks. That work has been dated at about 1810. Over 150 years later a ten-foot long butt-end lies on the ground adjacent to one stump: testimony not only to the preservative qualities of cedar but also on reflection, to stun the senses when you acknowledge the fact that such giants were felled without power saws or even modern axes.

But this is the true land of the war canoe, home

to an ancient and skilled civilization. That anyone could carve such giant canoes and propel them through the challenging channels and open waters that surround the island in order to raid neighbouring tribes also testifies to the natives' skill as seamen. Even today mariners consider these waters dangerous despite all the tools of modern navigation. Sudden squalls and endless fogs can roll in with little warning.

This is also part of the land of the totem pole; a symbol of history and status for each family or community. Today most such poles are seen in urban park settings or museums where they can be admired as an interesting artform. To appreciate the full power of the totem pole, however, encounter one unannounced among giant trees, on a hazy shoreline as it would have stood years ago by a fishing village. One such solitary pole stands at Winter Harbour. For splendid examples of indian art, however, visit Alert Bay on Cormorant Island a few miles east of Port McNeill. It is today's headquarters for the Kwakiutl arts and crafts and there are magnificent totems as well as examples of the long house.

The architectural and engineering skills of the ancient indians is difficult to appreciate fully in this era of skyscrapers. This region is where the post and beam architecture which imparts such a distinctive flavour to contemporary West Coast home design had its origins. The lodge houses of the coast indians were built with massive posts of cedar, dragged from the forest and stood on end. For roof support beams, massive cedar tree logs were hoisted atop the posts with a smaller log used for ridge pole.

Also to be seen, and treated with care so that future generations may enjoy them, are the ancient petroglyphs.

Most easily viewed are those at Petroglyph Park on the southern edge of the city of Nanaimo and at Sproat Lake Park near Port Alberni.

Symbols carved onto rock, the origin of the petroglyphs is not well-defined. Many are not representative of the culture of the present indian inhabitants of the northwest. They defy accurate dating and anthropologists have yet to resolve whether the oldest are of Polynesian or Asian origin or the work of an indigenous pre-indian people who have left no other traces from which their story can be reconstructed.

Petroglyph locations, of which more than thirty have been identified on Vancouver Island and adjacent islands, are now receiving protection even against well-intentioned visitors. The stone, usually sandstone, wears away easily.

The Archaeological and Historic Sites Protection Act provides for fines up to $1,000 and up to six months in jail for anyone who destroys, defaces or alters an indian painting or carving on rock.

Although some are of pre-historic origin, carving has been witnessed in isolated instances and carvings such as those of sailing ships and early steamers are obviously of relatively recent origin. Boas, a German anthropologist who studied the indians of the northwest, recorded that one petroglyph carving at Fort Rupert was made just prior to 1882. It commemorated the ritual eating of a slave within the memory of witnesses whom he was able to interview.

How long have men lived on this island? One archaeological site at Millard Creek near Courtenay has been dated at 6,350 B.C. Within the adjacent coastal region, dating has proceeded back as far as 8,000 B.C. There is a rich history here but one as yet largely undiscovered and unexplained.

This history can be shared by spending some time in the many museums and historical collections created in each community. At Nanaimo, for example, you can see the Hepburn Stone, a petroglyph found while excavating for a well...at a depth of 28 feet! It is on display at the Bastion.

Near Duncan is the Forest Museum, a collection of early-day, and more recent, logging and sawmilling equipment. Through interesting exhibits and artifacts the museum offers an education about the forest and the technology used. Included is a short trip on a railway with the train pulled by a restored logging locomotive.

Another major historical display is to be seen at the Kwakiutl Indian village at Alert Bay where ceremonial dances are performed for the entertainment, and enlightenment, of visitors.

Not everything worth seeing is situated by any means in such readily-accessible locations. Tsusiat Falls on the West Coast Lifesaving Trail is a rare sight, but you need to be a sturdy hiker to enjoy it. Plunging like a miniature Niagara over a steep rock face, the Tsusiat empties 60 feet onto the beach at low tide. At high tide it falls directly into the ocean, one of the few such falls in the world.

Also seen only by hikers is Canada's highest waterfall. Streaming 1,443 feet into Drinkwater River, Della Falls is one of the world's greatest falls. To reach it means a hike from Great Central Lake or an even longer and more difficult hike from Buttle Lake in Strathcona Park.

The majority of attractions on the island are however, readily shared by everyone. There are numerous parks, the two largest and most important being Pacific Rim National Park and Strathcona

The Sandpiper searches for its food along the
tideline of the island's beaches. A merry-looking seabird with
its bouncy walk, it is clannish and materializes as
a flock leaving just as swiftly if startled.

Provincial Park.

Pacific Rim comprises three sections along the island's central west coast and contains 35,280 acres of which 22,000 acres are land and almost 14,000 acres water.

The best known section is Long Beach, the 26-mile long northern portion of the park. Included is the unbroken 12-mile stretch of sand at Wickanninish Bay together with Grice Bay on Tofino Inlet and a portion of Kennedy Lake.

South of Long Beach on Ucluth Penninsula is Ucluelet, an active fishing village, with nearby Amphitrite Point Lighthouse. North of the park is Tofino, a logging and fishing community.

For those with a bent for history, a boatride will take you from Tofino to an American Fort on Meares Island. In 1791-92, Capt. Robert Gray aboard the *Columbia* wintered in Adventure Cove, building Fort Defiance as protection against any hostile indians. Long lost in the jungle-like coastal growth, Fort Defiance was rediscovered in 1966 by Ken Gibson of Tofino and is now being painstakingly restored.

Although prior British exploration denied the Americans sovereignty, Gray's ship was the original source from which British Columbia derived its name. What irony that a colony created to keep Americans from controlling the coast should indirectly adopt the nickname early Americans had given their nation.

Off Ucluelet, at the entrance to Alberni Inlet, is Barkley Sound with the second section of Pacific Rim National Park, the Broken Islands Group, and across the water, on the south shore, Bamfield, a fishing port. Nesting grounds for Sea Lions and sea birds, the islands form an oceanic preserve.

Now used as the base for a federal oceanic research station, Bamfield was originally famous for its Cable Station, built in 1902 as the North American end of the Trans-Pacific telegraphic cable. The cable next touched land 4,000 miles away at Fanning Island. Later the station was linked with Hawaii and the terminal relocated, in 1963, at Port Alberni.

Bamfield can be reached by small boat from Ucluelet or by logging road from Port Alberni. This road connects, via a 20-mile spur, onto Nitinat Lake. A tidal lake almost devoid of life because of its salinity, it forms a portion of the third section of Pacific Rim National Park which stretches from Pachena Point south to just above Port Renfrew and encompasses all of the old West Coast Life Saving Trail. Except for Nitinat Lake, this section of the park is accessible only on foot.

Pachena Bay, a short hike from Bamfield, is a popular beach and campsite area but the ocean is colder than most people can stand even for a short dip. Out on the headland is Pachena Light, counterpart to Amphitrite on the north shore of the entrance to Alberni Inlet. This stretch of the coast centres an area called the Graveyard of the Pacific for the number of ships it is known to have claimed over the years.

The Lifesaving Trail, now abandoned, was built in 1890 to enable survivors of wrecks to reach safety. A telegraph line was installed to connect the coast lighthouses and for many years it was the linesmen who maintained the trail.

Strathcona Park, a 530,319 acre preserve west of Campbell River, was created to protect a wildlife area and includes the highest group of mountain peaks on the island, Mt. Col. Foster at 7,000', Elkhorn at 7,191', and the highest of them all, Golden Hinde at 7,219'. They stand as sentinels guarding the western boundaries of the park which is home to a herd of Roosevelt Elk native to the island and once nearly pushed to extinction by hunters.

In the accessible portion of the park is all of Buttle Lake and most of Upper Campbell Lake, both swollen beyond their original size by Strathcona Dam. The dam with its companion John Hart Dam at Elk Falls at the outflow of Lower Campbell Lake, provides water storage for the island's largest hydro-electric generating system.

At the southern end of Buttle lake, some 20 miles from the main road, is the Western Mines operation at which, in summer, visitors wishing to take a tour are welcome.

Along the road to Campbell River is the Elk Falls paper mill operated by Crown Zellerbach Canada Ltd. Tours of this mill are also available each day in summer.

From Buttle Lake climbers can head into Forbidden Plateau and Mt. Albert Edward to the east or head south to visit Della Falls.

Strathcona, together with Elk Falls Park at the east end of Campbell Lake, is one of the island's largest and most popular vacation and recreational areas.

Campsites are plentiful except at the height of the summer tourist season and fishing in the area's numerous lakes is excellent.

Campbell River on the east coast is the commer-

The woods of Vancouver Island offer many colourful plants. The Tiger Lily (top left) and Trillium (top right) are found in forested areas, the skunk cabbage (lower right) in bogs and marshes. If you know where to look colourful mushrooms such as this poisonous Fly Agaric on Denman Island can also be found.

cial centre for the north east coastal areas as well as a world-famous tyee salmon fishing centre. Numerous resorts dot the highway and shoreline along nearby Discovery Passage, a narrow channel connecting Johnstone Strait and the Strait of Georgia. It is a channel almost solid with large and small islands.

In this narrow passage, a few miles north of Campbell River, is Seymour Narrows, site of the once-infamous Ripple Rock. Discovered by Captain Vancouver, the twin-peaked rock rose to within 10' of the surface at low tide. Ripple Rock tore the bottom out of many a hull and claimed scores of lives

The float house tucked away in a secluded spot is a popular summer cottage on lake and inlet. For many years logging camp communities on floats were commonplace. When cutting was completed they were towed to a new location.

Opposite page:
Abandoned farmland at Hansen's Lagoon. Now part of Cape Scott Provincial Park, the lagoon and San Josef Bay a few miles south, were settled by Danish immigrants at the turn of the century. Lack of access to markets caused the settlement to fail. Access today is only by sea or by trail, with the difficult trail suitable only for experienced hikers. A few wilderness campsites are available in the park.

until it was mined by tunneling beneath the sea. In 1958 it was blasted away to a depth of 47' by the world's largest ever non-nuclear explosion.

Smaller parks abound on the island, many of them including picnicking and camping facilities. Two of the best known Provincial Parks are Little Qualicum Falls and Englishmen's River on the road from the beach resort communities of Qualicum and Parksville to Port Alberni. Another, situated mid-way between Courtenay and Campbell River, is Miracle Beach park.

Parks large and small welcome visitors all over the island. The diversity is a real boon. Playground and picnic facilities have been provided by every community. Seeking out little known local parks can provide many days of rewarding activity.

Lake and river shores where swimming or fishing are possible have frequently been set aside and modestly equipped. Among these are Westwood Lake at Nanaimo, Sproat Lake, Comox Lake and Bright Angle, an exquisite maple and cedar thronged riverside park near Duncan approached across a cable-supported swinging bridge.

Equally charming is the black rock narrow gorge at Stamp Falls Park near Port Alberni. The river's pools are popular with steelhead fishermen. Here,

in early autumn, salmon can be observed leaping the falls or using the fishladder, one of the first such protective ladders built on an island river to try and improve the survival rate for the spawning salmon. In these river parks on a quiet day, deer can be seen drinking at the river edge and in the heat of summer sometimes even black bears searching for berries.

There are many seashore parks as well, especially at beach areas popular for swimming. Departure Bay in Nanaimo is one of the larger ones. Ivy Green south of Ladysmith is another, and one that affords fascinating exploration of flat tidelands for youngsters.

Probably the most popular of the oceanfront beaches is Rathtrevor Beach at Parksville. Once a private farm, Rathtrevor forms part of a beach area which extends along most of a ten-mile stretch ending north of Qualicum. But the portion from Parksville Bay to Rathtrevor has the broadest sands. Here the incoming tides slowly rise over sun-baked sand absorbing additional warmth. The almost flat beach is a giant sandbox safely enjoyed by any toddler.

One of the prettiest shoreline parks has recently been created at crescent-shaped Beaver Harbour near the Port Hardy townsite and encompassing the remnants of Fort Rupert. Quadra Island directly opposite Campbell River offers yet another kind of shoreline park at Rebecca Spit on the Southeastern shore and is a popular sheltered swimming area. Also on Quadra Island is the Octopus Islands Marine Park, accessible only by water. Immediately north is Sonora Island with its Thurston Bay Marine Park, again only reached by boat.

Different still is Nanaimo's offshore park, Newcastle Island. And the Gulf Islands which string along the eastern shore contain many parks including marine campsites for the enjoyment of the boating fraternity. Among the latter the largest and most popular is Montague Harbour on Galiano Island.

One reason for the large number of parks around the island is that motoring has always been a pleasure on the island. Even today, although traffic may choke main roads on occasion, an evening or weekend drive rewards a family with something for everyone's enjoyment. Each highway and by-way is scenic. The spots to explore seemingly infinite.

The principal thoroughfare, the Island Highway, is itself the main attraction following as it does along the eastern shore. In places, though, those who

know the island will choose to follow the twisting old highway in order to visit again many small communities and now out-of-the-way scenes bypassed as the main road was up-graded and straightened.

Especially worthwhile in that regard are the old roads through Cedar district south of Nanaimo, through Cowichan Bay and Mill Bay near Duncan and the Lantzville road north of Nanaimo.

Even more worthwhile are the logging roads which honeycomb almost all of the island's forested area. Two of these on the north island warrant special mention. One will be enjoyed by more people after the new northern sections of the Island Highway are completed, but the other, which was part of the earlier logging road route to Port Hardy, will be overlooked by all those drivers seeking the shortest route to their destination.

A beautiful drive, the latter is the old road from Beaver Cove alongside Bonanza Lake to Woss Camp. This road, mainly utilized by Crown Zellerbach with the shorter southern portion within the Canadian Forest Products Co. tree farm area, is an excellent example of high standard logging roads and is easily travelled by even light autos. The southern end now intersects with the new highway midway between Nimpkish Camp and Woss Camp.

Close to that intersection is another junction with a Canadian Forest Products' road leading to the southern end of the Nimpkish Valley. This now links up with the Thasis Co. road to Zeballos. The latter is one of the most spectacular roads on the island. When eventually brought up to highway standards it will prove a major tourist attraction offering scenery rivalled only in the Rockies.

Small Wolfe Lake provides the initial scenic interest on the Zeballos Road, then Pinder Peak at 5,060' and Mook Peak at 4,794'. But the first revelation comes at Mason Falls. In summer, four waterfalls cascade over the steep bare face of the mountain. Earlier in runoff time, additional smaller streams pour over the face. Even into summer, the mountain top can be capped with snow, with both snow and falls reflecting in the quiet pools below.

The road becomes more difficult as it climbs towards Zeballos Peak, 5,171', and then snakes its way down alongside the Zeballos River to Zeballos Inlet, a fjord-like spur off Esperanza Inlet. Although not recommended for the Sunday driver in its present state, the road is safe. Proceed with just a bit more caution than is usually warranted on all of the logging roads.

Apart from the thrill of motoring over a road that rivals the pre-World War II Fraser Canyon Road, the river is worth the trip. Alternating from smooth flowing broad channels and quiet pools the river tumbles over rapids and smashes over boulder strewn cascades as it fights its way to the sea. The road clings evenly to the canyon side while the river changes elevation in great plunges. So abrupt are the changes in the river's nature and colours that one cannot help but wonder if it is all the same river. At the estuary is the picturesque town of Zeballos, once a gold-mining town but now predominantly a logging community.

Two other beautiful drives, both along paved highways, can be found on the north and central island. Between Port Hardy and Port McNeill a highway runs to the pulp mill town of Port Alice on Neroutsos Inlet, an arm of Quatsino Sound. Along the way, the highway crosses the Marble River which connects Victoria Lake to Alice Lake. At the river crossing is one of the larger of many camping and picnicking sites created by the forest companies, in this instance Rayonier Canada (BC) Ltd., to permit greater enjoyment of the forest lands by everyone.

The other notable drive is from Port Alberni to Long Beach. This road to the West Coast runs alongside the Somass River, crosses Sproat River and then parallels the shore of Sproat Lake, one of the island's prettiest. At the end of the lake, in autumn, salmon cram the Taylor River to spawn, a sight well worth stopping to enjoy. Wending through the forest highlands again the road crosses behind Mt. Klitsa then follows the Kennedy River to the island's largest lake, Kennedy, which at an elevation of only 22' is almost an arm of the Pacific.

Motorists seeking more pastoral drives head for the Comox and Cowichan Valleys. Both long-established agricultural areas each has many miles of sideroads running through gently undulating landscapes interlaced with creeks. At harvest time, these valleys offer a tranquility drastically at odds with the wild lands. They also impart a feeling of permanence absent in much of the island. That same permanence is found as well on the Gulf Islands, such as Saturna, where sheep graze on lands settled for well over a hundred years.

It is when autumn turns the leaves of the lower hillsides and these valleys to yellow and once in awhile to scarlet that the island shows its most gentle nature.

It is an irresistible snare.

The inter-tidal zone reveals colourful starfish clinging to the rocks at low tide. Tidal pools are filled with anemonies, small crabs and often tiny fish to elude the hands of small children while providing an absorbing pastime. The tranquility of the island's sandy coves is portrayed (above) at Guise Bay near the north end of the island.

Walking the log is a required skill for hikers on Vancouver Island as fallen trees often provide the only means to cross rivers, streams and ravines. Above a party of hikers crosses Fishermen's River.

The outdoors beckons constantly and young people, even in town, can always find a hike within their capability. This group enjoys a close-up view of falls on the Darling River. The scarlet daub of Indian Paintbrush (below) adds contrast to meadows and roadside greenery.

The thrill of success rewards a paddler mastering the Cowichan River rapids near Duncan in a kayak. For those who climb mountains the friendly Whiskey-jack (Canada Jay) is a companion who stays close . . . to plunder food. Spring brings the multi-hued crocus to island gardens with a late snowfall creating a conflict of seasons for gardeners.

The lowland fields and upland trails provide the horseback rider with room to roam. Beaches such as Croteau Beach at Comox are popular for riding when not crowded with summer swimmers. An Oxeye Daisy basks in the summer sun. Daisies grow wild in many parts of the island. The delicate Columbine (Aquilegia) (below) is one of many wild flowers native to the island.

Doughty trawlers and giant freighters share the fjord-like water-ways and narrow channels. Above: Freighter in-bound to load lumber at Port Alberni.

The sea constantly changes mood. On rocky shores swirling surf foams and surges cleansing the shore or hurling driftwood yet higher above the tideline.

Preceding pages: Wildflowers singly and in profusion are one of the joys of the island's woodlands and meadows. At the top left the glossy green and red leaves of an Oregon Grape add colour to a rocky slope along with the soft purple blossoms of wild Delphiniums. Symbol of Easter-time is the delicate Dog-toothed Violet (top right) which grows wild in the woodlands. More often seen is the white variety. The mauve-pink thistle, (lower left) is plentiful but the shy Pink Slipper orchid (lower right) must be searched out.

On Hornby Island summer brings a host of flowers.

Most lakes and streams on the island will provide a good catch and a chance for father and son (above) to share a day's companionship in the sunshine. At right is one of the numerous waterfalls which add to the beauty of the island's lakes. This is Myra Falls on Buttle Lake.

The clean deep waters of twenty-two mile long Great Central Lake, opposite page, near Port Alberni attract fishermen, water skiers and boaters. Tucked into many bays are float houses which serve as summer homes. They range in size from tiny box-like cabins to ample two-storey residences. The water in some streams feeding the lake, such as McBride Creek, is so pure they will not support fish life.

Friendly Cove, Nootka Island, was the landing place for British Captain James Cook in 1778, the first European to step ashore on the northwest coast. His vessel, "H.M.S. Discovery", was accompanied by "H.M.S. Resolution".

The cove, site of Chief Maquinna's summer headquarters, continued as a trading centre of importance for half a century.

In 1886, Captain John Meares sailed from Calcutta aboard the "Nootka" and built the "Northwest America" at the cove. It was commandeered by the Spaniard Martinez in 1789 along with two other ships. The Spanish built a base at the cove.

Captain George Vancouver arrived in 1793 and, under the Nootka Agreement, regained possession for Britain.

Named by Cook because of the welcome he received from the Nootka people, Friendly Cove now greets an ever-increasing flow of visitors from around the world. The "Uchuck III" provides summer excursions to the historic village from Gold River, once Maquinna's winter headquarters.

Woodland trails are everywhere to entice young and old for a stroll. Above is Bowen Park in Nanaimo.

Nanaimo Yacht Club and municipal park, (above right) provide this tranquil setting only a short distance from the Hub City's bustling commercial centre.

Even a walk through residential areas can be rewarding to the eye. At right is a picturesque thatched-roof cottage in Comox. Craftsmen from Britain were imported to build early homes opening a path that is followed by some even today.

Many roads on Vancouver Island were originally constructed for logging purposes, as was this road to Franklin River west of Port Alberni. As logging activity intensified, the network of roads extended further into the forest areas opening up many scenic and recreational attractions.

Some of the early logging roads have been reclassified as public roads but the majority remain private roads. To provide increased public access the forest companies have opened almost all of their roads using a standard system of marking to inform motorists of the status of each road. The companies also publish maps of their road systems and information on attractions and about camp sites, picnic areas and boat launching ramps which they have developed in a great many locations.

The standard marking system uses a green sign to indicate roads not in active use and which are open to the public 24 hours a day; a yellow caution sign for roads which, while also open, may still be in use by heavy equipment; and red for roads in active logging use. The latter are open only outside of working hours. Local enquiry is recommended.

Nocturnal Racoons are not shy and can become pests. Their bandit markings signify their willingness to steal food. They, and the cheerful Squirrels, are among the most often seen forest creatures that inhabit the island.

Deer are plentiful on the island although smaller than their mainland cousins. Back roads near streams at evening provide the best chance for a look at these shy animals.

Looking for directions, like any other sailor, this seal decided to take a closer look at a bell buoy in Porlier Pass.

The mildest winters in Canada are enjoyed by residents of the southeastern coast of Vancouver Island and the adjacent Gulf Islands. The warming Japanese current moderates the climate of the entire island.

Islanders joke about the amount of rainfall in some west and north coast areas, such as Henderson Lake where the annual 264" qualifies it as the second rainiest place on earth. There are dry areas with light rainfall on the east coast: Parksville with 200 dry days and only 37.5" per year and Duncan with an average of 38". On the Gulf Islands, rainfall drops as low as an average of 30" at Pender Island.

Still the frosts of winter do come for a few days in most years creating a snow and ice wonderland all the more enjoyable for its brevity.

Saltwater seldom freezes near the island but small coves with a top layer of fresh water from a creek will freeze over occasionally as did this one near Chemainus.

Beauty can be found even in the dullest of winter days. Photo at right, taken at Sointula, captures the quiet of twilight.

Busily paddling to keep their bit of open water clear of ice are two ducks. Many waterfowl winter on Vancouver Island, testimony to the general mildness of its winters.

Living on Tomorrow Island

Vancouver Island is essentially a young person's country. Large areas remain frontier of a kind. Wherever you turn the youthful exuberance of the citizenry is evident and children plentiful.

The young find good incomes from employment in the island's industries. The future is promising. The people exude a refreshing confidence secure in the knlowledge that each community can be developed as they wish it to be. The towns of the island reflect that positive approach to life, an approach that has now spanned several generations and which is contagious among recent arrivals.

Though numerically less evident, there are plenty of old-folks who have enjoyed a lifetime on the island. With them to share the mild winters are large numbers who retired to the island from the prairies and from Eastern Canada where winter can be harsh. To credit the climate, or the scenery, with attracting retired persons to Vancouver Island glosses over an even more important fact of island life.

Vancouver Islanders are a sociable people. The unsociable are genuine exceptions. But even the unsociable are more than simply tolerated. The island has had its share of hermits and recluses and today solitary characters are still plentiful. It is a place where people are prepared to mind their own business — after making overtures of hospitality or neighbourliness.

Social patterns still partially reflect the early day needs of frontier people to look after each other. Few islanders will pass up an opportunity to help anyone in need of assistance. Most will go far out of their way to help.

Community activities are numerous and any holiday will provide a choice of entertainment; a gymkhana, a parade, a fair, a pageant, a logger's sports competition.

Nanaimo has held a Victoria Day celebration (which they resolutely call Empire Day) each May 24th weekend for 107 years. July 1st, the anniversary of Canadian Confederation in 1867, is celebrated in several towns, each competing with the other to attract greater crowds. And Labour Day, an important event in most island towns because of the long history of strong unionism, adds to the colour of the year's happenings.

Thrown in for zest are the special events. The zanier the better. Topping that list is Nanaimo's annual Bathtub Race, established in 1967. Competitors from around the world vie with each other to cross Georgia Strait, a distance of 32 miles. The majority of entrants swamp at the starting line year after year.

At Duncan every Labour Day weekend indians from B.C. and Washington State communities compete in war canoe races. Most years the indians also stage their own sports competitions at nearby Cowichan Bay.

But these are just the surface activities. Each is founded upon a carefully nurtured community spirit, a spirit that has built sports facilities, community halls, churches, schools and hospitals of high standards.

Port Hardy sports a modern hospital. But Alert Bay on nearby Cormorant Island has provided hospital care to the sick and needy of the north island and up-coast areas since 1870.

Duncan has a modern recreation centre. But nearby Cowichan Bay has the South Cowichan Lawn Tennis Club, in continuous operation, at the same site, since 1884.

Each is a mark of pride in the community and the symbol of a willingness to build for the future as well as for today. That pride is a major reason for the continuing progress that marks all areas

of the island. Important as they are, however, these urban facilities do not begin to explain the enthusiasm for life shared by island residents of all ages.

It is the outdoors that captivate most Vancouver Islanders. Hiking and climbing beckon all the young people into the hills and trails creating a habit that remains for life.

Boating, always popular because of fishing, has in recent years come into its own, especially on the East Coast where the protected waters between Vancouver Island and the Gulf Islands afford excellent sailing and power boating: an ocean playground with few equals in the world.

Marinas have sprung up in most island communities, certainly in all those with any natural protected moorage. Over the years the government has built numerous breakwaters to create additional safe moorage. Roads are dotted with boat launching ramps.

While it is taken for granted on the island, visitors are amazed at the way a boat owner will moor his craft in a salt water fishing area and casually pick it up and trailer it for a day's lake fishing or boating. It is easily done, but few areas of the world offer such a selection of waters to cruise or fish within only a few miles of each other.

To gain an appreciation of the number of families who own boats, don't just look at the marinas, look in the driveways and carports of the homes. Small craft are parked everywhere.

Sport fishing is immensely popular and because of proximity of ocean, lake and stream to their homes, many residents are able to get in some fishing after supper from spring through to fall. Dedicated sportsmen fish all winter, seeking the fighting steelhead trout.

Fresh water fishing offers Cutthroat, Brown,

Hawaii is 2500 miles across the open Pacific from world-famous Long Beach, (above). Now part of Pacific Rim National Park, the 12-mile stretch of hard-packed sand is one of the longest in the world and was considered in the 1930's by Britain's Sir Malcolm Campbell as a site for an attempt on the world's auto speed record. Now closed to cars, the beach has buried many an auto as incoming tides turned the sand soft.

Sweeping views of the inner island, the coast or the nearby mainland reward climbers tackling the island's mountains. This youth, resting high up on Mount Cain, enjoys a bird's-eye view of logging roads in the valley below.

Rainbow and Kamloops trout plus bass and the much-prized Steelhead, a sea-run trout considered the gamest of all, and the tastiest.

The ocean offers up salmon in a variety of shapes and sizes from grilse, of approximately twelve inches, to blueback, a Coho salmon weighing two to six pounds, and the Spring salmon all the way up to the Tyee, the adult fish which returns in the fall and weighs from twenty-five to over seventy pounds. Spring salmon can be taken year round. Along the shores, cod, sole and pink snapper.

Children seem to be born with fishing rods in hand. On bridges near tidewater youngsters of all sizes try for a catch. On piers and floats small-fry practice on perch, bullheads and minnows with a bent pin and string. When the salmon are running motorists waiting for a ferry at Mill Bay can watch as a surf-casting teen-ager lands a 26 pound salmon. At Campbell River the government wharf is lined with scores of anglers in season, all after Tyee. Is it any wonder that a non-fisherman is a rarity on the island?

Despite this widespread interest in fishing, it is still quite easy to find yourself the only fisherman on a lake or stream because there are so many fishing spots. In areas distant from the larger communities, it is possible to fish totally undisturbed with your only companion a loon or a heron, themselves skilled at fishing.

Beaches are largely uncrowded in summer, as are ski slopes in winter, compared to similar facilities in the province's lower mainland area.

Skiing on the island has been popular for many years with Forbidden Plateau near Courtenay the first area developed for downhill skiers. Mount Arrowsmith, long the most promising area but difficult to reach for many years, was finally developed in 1975 and now offers good facilities and tows. The third major skiing area is Green Mountain, south of Nanaimo.

Although attention now focuses on the downhill facilities, the island's mountains have beckoned cross-country skiers for a longer time, as logged-over hillsides, and the unused logging roads themselves, provide excellent trails and runs.

Golf is popular on the island. Private and public courses are found in most areas. With the mild winters, it is a sport that can be played year-round.

Tennis is an equally popular island sport, and again, public courts are plentiful. Curling, which enjoyed an enormous boom on the island in the late 1950's, remains popular and rinks exist in all the larger communities. With the wide availability of artificial ice, two new sports came to the island: skating and ice

hockey. Given the mild winter, earlier generations just didn't find it practical to invest in skating gear on the off-chance that a lake might freeze solid enough for skating.

The English influence, which is so strong in Victoria, crops up in island sports with soccer, lawn bowling, croquet, grass hockey and, at Duncan and Nanaimo, the occasional cricket match.

Almost everywhere is to be found a well-cared for ball field and you can be sure that there are community teams playing softball or baseball regularly with teams from neighbouring communities. The inter-community rivalry — and shared socializing — is quite marked.

Although the larger urban centres are much more self-contained, the pattern of visiting back and forth to other communities continues. Many residents of Duncan, Nanaimo, Port Alberni, Courtenay and Campbell River have lived or worked in the smaller centres and have friends there.

For the most part, the towns of Vancouver Island have a raw newness of look to them because so

much of the growth in even the established communities has occurred in the past 30 years.

On maps of the island, marked communities may consist of only a handful of homes. These are the mining and logging camp communities and indian villages of by-gone days. For many years as logging in an area shut down, perhaps for 60 or more years until a new crop of trees grew, the loggers and their families moved on to a new location. Mining also added its share of abandoned communities.

In many instances a few families stayed to fish, hunt, work on road maintenance, run a service station, corner store or to farm. These people count among the real pioneers of the island for they were not transients who just happened to live in that spot. These were people who chose it. Life may have been tough at times, but these islanders were tough persistent people and not easily beaten by the weather, the forest or lack of

The island's west coast trail area (above) affords magnificent scenery to those capable of the rugged hike.

Lakes dot the island providing excellent recreation and fishing throughout the year. This scene is at the mouth of Phillips Creek on Buttle Lake.

money. Like the forest giants they took root on the rockiest soil, survived and eventually prospered.

There is a streak of that doggedness in most islanders. As a result, considerable numbers of young couples will be found building their own summer cabins, or clearing land and building homes. Even in the settled cities evidence of that continual drive to build and to tame the land is all around you. So it is that at the pulp mill town of Port Alice you will find well-cared for lawns and gardens. Indeed, evidence of gardening is seen along all the streets of the towns and magnificent testimonies to patience and a generous climate can be enjoyed.

Here on the island the urge to own land in order to ensure both independence and the chance at fuller enjoyment of the individual's chosen life-style is very strong. The young dream not of an apartment or suburban home but of acreage or land by a river or lake. They may live in town, but a piece of their heart is in the forest or on the seashore and it is that returning to which they look forward.

The amounts of money islanders will spend on boats, campers, tents, trailers or whatever equipment they need to pursue their outdoor

interests is substantial. And automobiles. For many of the most interesting places can be reached only by private vehicle or boat . . . plus a hike. Public transport is largely limited to the main roads.

But there was a day of the railway. In 1886, the Esquimalt and Nanaimo Railway, built by Dunsmuir, was completed from Victoria to Nanaimo. Acquired by the C.P.R. in 1906, the E&N service was extended to Port Alberni in 1911 and later to Courtenay. Use declined after World War II and passenger service is now only operating on the original line.

A persistent dream of the islanders was a rail connection to the mainland using island-hopping bridges or tunnels in the Seymour Narrows area. As recently as the 1950's such proposals continued to come forward every few years. But in the post-war years the dominance of the automobile became complete; the railway faded in importance and the attention of the dreamers turned to auto ferries and auto bridges. Passenger service now is close to non-existent although freight trains still shuffle on the E & N right-of-ways.

From the earliest recorded history, island communities were linked by boat. For many years, the

Canadian Pacific Steamship Company provided service to the west coast settlements out of Victoria. The most famous vessel on the run was the *Princess Maquinna*. Its arrival in town was an event that drew everyone to the waterfront because it carried not only food and other supplies, it carried mail and visitors.

Aircraft made possible faster passenger and mail service. The burgeoning highway network removed sea-borne traffic to the larger communities and made short haul land transport practical so that the steamship service was gradually replaced by small coastal shipping services. Some of these continue to operate today. Among the major ones is the *M.V. Lady Rose* which provides daily service between Ucluelet and Bamfield. Operated out of Port Alberni, the *Lady Rose* turns tourist in summer to carry thousands of visitors out to the Pacific through the 42-mile fjord-like inlet that nearly bisects the island.

Its predecessor on the Alberni Inlet, *M.V. Uchuck III*, now serves the Nootka Sound area with Gold River at the head of Muchalat Inlet as home port. It runs up Tahsis and Zeballos Inlets, providing those communities with reliable year round service. In summer, *Uchuck III* also provides visitors

with a chance to see the magnificent west coast scenery and is the water link to historic Friendly Cove on Nootka Sound.

For other communities such as Mahatta River and Quatsino on Quatsino Sound, logging company ships make regular visits. To travel on these, however, special arrangements are required.

Apart from the excursion boats, and small craft

A dramatic rescue underway during Nanaimo's world-famous annual Bath Tub Race. Such rescues are often carried out by escort boats, which each competitor must have in recognition of the fact that a majority of the competitors do not finish the race each year.

Opposite Page:
Axe-throwing, tree-climbing, log-rolling, falling and bucking competitions are all among the loggers' sports featured in many island community events, such as this one at Ucluelet.

Water skiing is enormously popular on the island because of the long season. The skiier in seeming solitude practices on Brannan Lake, only a few miles from the busy city of Nanaimo.

which can be chartered in many communities for saltwater fishing, visitors still savour the voyage to and from the island as most traffic is carried on auto ferries which link the island to the mainland. Large, efficient and generally maintaining frequent schedules, these ferries are the successors to the early steamships.

Aiding them in providing island residents with contact to the mainland are scheduled airline services from modern airports at Port Hardy, Comox, Nanaimo, Patricia Bay near Victoria, and Tofino. Smaller airports provide land-based service from almost all other communities, but the island is also well-served by water-based float planes both charter and schedule.

Transport on the island and to the mainland is now an easy matter and with rare exceptions impervious to disruption by winter storms. Communication with the world is simple. Near Duncan is one of Canada's satellite communications stations, a successor and supplement to the Trans-Pacific cable.

Yet despite these modern amenities which bring the world into instant contact and closeness, the island remains different and its people different.

Even after conceding the influence of the generous outdoors on everyone's way of life, a difference remains. After conceding the importance of its mild climate, a style remains that is not explained by the seeming isolation of an island.

The answer is to be found in the ever-changing sunsets which shed glory in the island skies. And in the sunrises. Both hold forth a promise: To-morrow will be better yet.

Incredible as that may seem, given the bounty of today on Vancouver Island, that is its secret.

This is tomorrow island.

To enter it fully, the island demands of each new arrival an initiation rite of many sunsets wit-nessed. Once entered the island holds each spirit captive, yet content, behind its war canoes. For there is freedom behind the war canoes.

"Freedom is everything ... beauty, happiness, life itself.
When it is ours ... we tend to take it for granted.
When it is lost ... we must fight to regain it.
For without it ... there is reason for nothing".[1]

1 *Gloria D. Czegledi, 1976.*

The only means across the tidal narrows of Nitinat Lake is by boat. Above, hikers are ferried by Bob Joseph of Wyack, last resident of this once-important indian fortress which defended the Nootka against invading Haidas.

More like a scene from a South seas island than its true location, photo at left shows a lean-to shelter erected at Cape Scott Provincial Park. This small dunes area at the northwest tip of the island has the characteristics of a desert.

Wherever you are, nothing beats a dinner of campfire-cooked, fresh-caught, fish.

Hiking on the island can present a variety of conditions. Sometimes the island trails are muddy from rain, as the young hiker below indicates. At day's end the companionship of the campfire meal more than makes up for the trials of the day, even on the rugged trails of the west coast (above) and at Cape Scott (below).

Photographic Credits

Front Cover (Dust Jacket): Night view of small craft harbour and fishing boats, Nanaimo - Glen MacRae, White Rock.

Back Cover (Dust Jacket): Walking on Long Beach at sundown - Hank Wilkinson, Duncan.

Front end paper: Waves at Wickaninnish Inn, Long Beach - Colin Knecht, Nanaimo.

Overleaf front end paper; Sailboat, Schooner Cove - Bill Inkster, Lantzville.

2 Shoreline, Guise Bay, near Cape Scott - Richard Brown, Port Hardy.

4 Boys on raft, Vernon Camp, Vernon Lake - Gloria Czegledi, Comox.

5 Boatman crossing the Nitinat bar - Donn Gardner, Nanaimo.

6 Birches reflected, Jingle Pot Road, Nanaimo - Doug Anderson, Nanaimo.

7 Young hiker climbing stairs to Cape Scott lighthouse - Donn Gardner, Nanaimo.

8 Mountains - Jim Peirson, Nanaimo.

10 Costumed Indian father and child at Alert Bay - Alf Flett, Nanaimo.

12 Mount Arrowsmith - Colin Knecht, Nanaimo.

14 Butter Church - Roy Herman, Nanaimo.

14 Chinatown, Duncan - Joyce Folbigg, Victoria.

15 Harvesting, Cowichan Bay - Alf Flett, Nanaimo.

16 Old Store - Eugene Cameron, Sayward.
Church - Theda Mackie, Vancouver.

17 Totem Pole - Joyce Folbigg, Victoria.

18 Old barn door - Donna Windecker, Nanaimo.

19 Cumberland village - Joyce Folbigg, Victoria.

20 Wedding - Donn Gardner, Nanaimo.
Roses in chapel - Doug Anderson, Nanaimo.

21 Sailboat at wharf - Daphne Pollard, Brentwood Bay.
Indian lady and child - Ron Burley, Ucluelet.

22 Table and chairs, Quatsino - Richard Brown, Port Hardy.

23 Haymower in barn, Cape Scott - Donn Gardner, Nanaimo.

24 Trail - Richard Brown, Port Hardy.
Locomotive - Jack Lindsay, Vancouver (Courtesy of Council of Forest Industries of B.C.)
Water Bomber - William Wainwright, Sproat Lake.

25 Loggers - (Courtesy of Crown Zellerbach Canada Ltd.)

26 Dozer boats, Cowichan Bay - George Kellett, Shawnigan Lake.

28 Paper mill - Jenny McCartney, Victoria.

29 Freighter loading - Donna Windecker, Nanaimo.

30 Bastion - Donn Gardner, Nanaimo.

33 Mobile spar tree - Jos. VanPoederooyen, Port Alberni.

34 Island Copper Mine at Rupert Inlet - Brian Kyle, Campbell River.

35 Open pit mining - Richard Brown, Port Hardy.

36 Pulp mill - Gloria Czegledi, Comox.

37 Wheel, Guise Bay, Cape Scott - Richard Brown, Port Hardy.
Tug boat - Richard Brown, Port Hardy.

38 Fishboat - Brian Biddlecombe, North Vancouver.

40 Whaling station - Ken Flett, Parksville.
Fisherman, Barkley Sound - Robert Kirk, Denman Island.

41 Whale watching, Tofino - Ken Budd, Tofino.

42 "Tofino - 5:00 a.m." - Brian Biddlecombe, North Vancouver.

44 Logging, Shawnigan Division of MacMillan & Bloedel near Duncan - Don Graham, Nanaimo.
Clam gathering - Ucluelet Inlet - Ron Burley, Ucluelet.

45 Pulp mill - Paul De Groot, Parksville.
Millyard - Ken Bowden, Shawnigan Lake.

46 Yacht - Lloyd Wood, Duncan.
Wilderness stream - John Simeon, Cowichan Station.
Canada Geese - Ken Bowden, Shawnigan Lake.

47 Arran Rapids, off Stuart Island northeast of Campbell River - Lloyd Wood, Duncan.

48 Fishnet, Johnstone Strait near Blinkhorn - Denise Peterson, Sointula.

Morning brings a variety of reflections to the calm waters of Winter Harbour (opposite). Typical of many island inlets which meander inland for miles, Winter Harbour is a base for fishermen and for a logging operation. Shed on float covers an engine and winch at an inactive log dump of the W. D. Moore Logging Company.

Acknowledgements

Foremost among those who have made this book possible were the photographers. Through their diverse insights we all share Vancouver Island as seen by those who love it and live there.

Many others contributed to the book, and we thank each one whether their contribution was a bit of history, a phrase, a comment on the photographs offered, or simply that wonderful thing... a word of encouragement. Each helped to make it possible. So did a collection of proud craftsmen:

Designed by Alfred Penz, Vancouver

Printed by Broadway Printers Ltd., Vancouver

Photographic technical services by
Commercial Illustrators Ltd., Vancouver

Bound by Vancouver Bookbinding Ltd., Vancouver

Production coordination and editing by
Meek Wilson Ltd., Vancouver

A special word of thanks is necessary for the contribution made by the judges in the Board's photographic competition which started the V.I.R.E.B. collection of island photos from which most of the selections were made. They were Glenn Christiansen, Chief of Photography, Sunset Magazine, Menlo Park, Calif., Arlen Bernie, Technical Representative, Kodak Ltd., Vancouver, and former professional photographer Archie Waldref, now a real estate agent with Totem Realty, Campbell River, B.C.

Singular contributions were also made by Richard Blockberger, Jake Veskoja and the chairman of the Board's public relations committee, Clair Wilson, together with Donn Gardner, Susan Piper and other members of the staff of Vancouver Island Real Estate Board.

But no one is more responsible than those who pioneered and built Vancouver Island into what it is today. To them we owe everything.

Dennis O'Leary, President,
Vancouver Island Real Estate Board

Slender Cormorants stand watch atop pilings near Campbell River harbour.
Opposite: Cape Mudge lighthouse.